Text in this format copyright © 1992 by Ideals Publishing Corporation
Illustrations copyright © 1992 by Carol Heyer

Published by Ideals Publishing Corporation
Nashville, Tennessee 37210

Printed and bound in the United States of America.

Library of Congress Cataloging-in-Publication Data

Alexander, Cecil Frances, 1818-1895
All things bright and beautiful / by Cecil Alexander; illustrated
by Carol Heyer.
p.   cm.
Summary: The words of the well-known hymn reflect God's creation of
animals, flowers, mountains, sun, rivers, humans, and our ability to
enjoy all that He made.
ISBN 0-8249-8544-3
1. Nature—Religious aspects—Christianity—Juvenile literature.
2. Creation—Juvenile literature. 3. Hymns, English—Juvenile
literature. [1. Nature—Songs and music. 2. Creation—Songs and
music. 3. Hymns.] I. Heyer, Carol, 1950- ill. II. Title.
BV353.A44   1992
264'.2—dc20   91-28428
                                                  CIP
                                                  AC

For my editor, Peggy Schaefer, for always believing in me and my
art. . . and for all my friends at Ideals Publishing Corporation.
                                                  - C.A.H.

Thanks to models:
    Joy Chu
    Max Chu Watson
    Kimberly Riggan

The illustrations in this book were rendered in felt-tipped pens.
The type was set in Palatino.
Color separations were made by Web Tech, Inc., Butler,
Wisconsin.
Printed and bound by Worzalla Publishing, Stevens Point,
Wisconsin.

Designed by Joy Chu.

CECIL FRANCES ALEXANDER

All Things Bright and Beautiful

Illustrated by

CAROL HEYER

Ideals Children's Books   *Nashville, Tennessee*

All things bright and beautiful,

All creatures great and small,

All things wise and wonderful,

The Lord God made them all.

Each little flower that opens,

Each little bird that sings,

He made their glowing colors,

He made their tiny wings;

The purple-headed mountain,

The river running by,

The sunset and the morning

That brightens up the sky;

The cold wind in the winter,

The pleasant summer sun,

The ripe fruits in the garden—

He made them every one.

The tall trees in the greenwood,

The meadows where we play,

The rushes by the water

We gather every day.

He gave us eyes to see them,

And lips that we might tell

How great is God Almighty

Who has made all things well!